D1636370

A Love Story Beginning in Spanish

For Kate Forhan,

With gratitude for
your support of
Tanya and wishing
you a wonderful
new journey.

in friendship,

Judith Ortiz Cofer
2/9/05

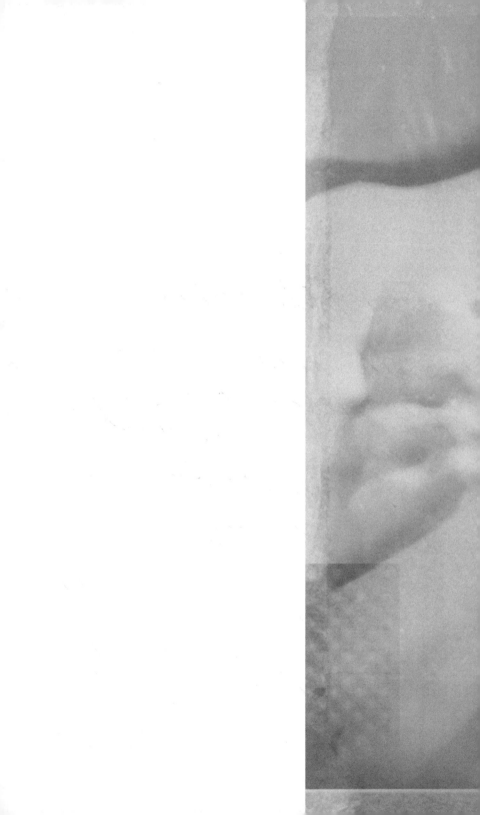

Poems by Judith Ortiz Cofer

A LOVE STORY

BEGINNING

IN SPANISH

The University of Georgia Press Athens and London

Published by The University of Georgia Press

Athens, Georgia 30602

© 2005 by Judith Ortiz Cofer

All rights reserved

Designed by Mindy Basinger Hill

Set in 10.5/13 Monotype Bulmer

Printed and bound by Thomson-Shore

The paper in this book meets the guidelines for

permanence and durability of the Committee on

Production Guidelines for Book Longevity of the

Council on Library Resources.

Printed in the United States of America

10 09 08 07 06 P 6 5 4 3 2

Library of Congress Cataloging-in-Publication Data

Ortiz Cofer, Judith, 1952–

A love story beginning in Spanish : poems / by Judith Ortiz Cofer.

p.   cm.

Includes bibliographical references.

ISBN 0-8203-2742-5 (pbk. : alk. paper)

I. Title.

PS3565.R7737L68 2005

811'.54—dc22   2005002716

ISBN-13 978-0-8203-2742-6 (pbk. : alk. paper)

British Library Cataloging-in-Publication Data available

You invaded my country by accident,

not knowing you had crossed the border.

DENISE LEVERTOV, "WAYS OF CONQUEST"

CONTENTS

ACKNOWLEDGMENTS

The American Voice: "Found Poem: Charm for the Love of a Woman," in Tenth Anniversary Issue, no. 37 (1995).

Americas Review: "That Old Tune," in vol. 19, no. 1 (1991); "La Fulana" as "Fulana," in vol. 16, no. 2 (1988) [reprinted in *Hispanic, Female, and Young*, Houston: Piñata Books, University of Houston, 1994.].

The Chattahoochee Review: "Where You Need to Go," in vol. 16, no. 4 (Summer 1996) [reprinted with a Spanish translation as "Donde necesitas ir," in *El Boletín de la Fundación Federico García Lorca*, año 9, no. 18 (diciembre de 1995), and in *Georgia Voices*, vol. 3, ed. Hugh Ruppersburg (Athens: University of Georgia Press, 2000)].

Colorado Review: "Black Silk Shirt" and "Saint, Hair, Water," in vol. 31, no. 2 (1994).

Georgia Review: "Lessons of the Past," in vol. 43, no. 1 (1989) [reprinted in *Indiana Review*, vol. 14, no. 3 (1991)].

Kenyon Review: "Notes for My Daughter Studying Math on the Morning of a New Year," in vol. 20, no. 3/4 (Summer/Fall 1998); "The Lesson of the Tongue," in vol. 13, no. 4 (1991).

The Latin Deli: Prose and Poetry by Judith Ortiz Cofer (Athens: University of Georgia Press: 1993): an earlier version of "Old Women in Their Rooms" as "Old Women."

New Letters: "Before the Storm," in vol. 65, no. 4 [reprinted in *El Coro: A Chorus of Latin and Latino Poetry*, ed. Martin Espada (Amherst: University of Massachusetts Press, 1997) and in *Georgia Voices*, vol. 3, ed. Hugh Ruppersburg (Athens: University of Georgia Press, 2000)].

Nightsun: "Siempre," in no. 23 (Fall 2004).

Prairie Schooner: "Bed-Making in a Foreign Country," "The Pleasures of Fear," and "The Gift of a Knife," in vol. 72, no. 4 (1998); "Here Is a Picture of Me," in vol. 74 (Summer 2000); "Beans: An Apologia for Not Loving to Cook," in vol. 75, no. 3 (2001). Forthcoming: "The Art of Scrying: A Poem for My Birthday" and "Rice: An Ars Poetica."

Silent Dancing: A Partial Remembrance of a Puerto Rican Childhood, essays and poems by Judith Ortiz Cofer (Houston: Arte Público Press, University of Houston, 1990): "Lessons of the Past," "That Old Tune," and "La Fulana" as "Fulana."

Snake Nation Review: "Alms Outside the Package Store, Peachtree Street," in vol. 2 (1990).

Southern Review: "First Job: The Southern Sweets Sandwich Shop and Bakery," in Special Issue on Contemporary Southern Poetry, vol. 30, no. 4 (1994) [reprinted in *Georgia Voices*, vol. 3, ed. Hugh Ruppersburg (Athens: University of Georgia Press, 2000)].

Southern Poetry Review: "Old Women in Their Rooms" as "Old Women," in vol. 27, no. 2 (1987) [reprinted in *Articulations: The Body and Illness in Poetry* (Iowa City: University of Iowa Press, 1994)]; "The Cruel Season" as "What We Feared," in vol. 26, no. 2 (1986).

Sudden Stories: The Mammoth Book of Miniscule Fiction, ed. Dinty W. Moore (DuBois, Pa.: Mammoth Books, 2003): "*El Amor*: A Story Beginning in Spanish" and "The Arms of a Good Woman."

To Mend the World: Women Reflect on 9/11, ed. Betty Jean Craige and Marjorie Agosín (Buffalo, N.Y.: White Pines Press, 2002): "The Names of the Dead: An Essay on the Phrase."

The Vestal Review, an online journal, in vol. 14, July 2003: "Hispanic Barbie with Accessories."

The Watershed Anthology II (LaCrosse: University of Wisconsin Press, 1999): "A Theory of Chaos: October 1962."

Witness: "Gifts" and "Dominoes," Fall 2003 (special issue, *On Ethnic America*).

Woman in Front of the Sun: On Becoming a Writer, essays and poems by Judith Ortiz Cofer (Athens: University of Georgia Press, 2000): "To Understand *El Azul*" and "Before the Storm."

Zone 3: "Seizing the Day," in vol. 2, no. 1 (1987).

Sections from A Sailor's Wife's Journal *originally published as individual poems*:
    Southern Review: section 1 as "Penelope," section 2 as "Dear Odysseus," in vol. 23, no. 4 (1987).
    The Kenyon Review: section 3 as "Learning to Walk Alone," section 4, "Lines for the Drowned Sailor Washed Ashore" as "The Drowned Sailor," in vol. 10, no. 4 (1988) [section 3 as "Learning to Walk Alone" also reprinted in *Anthology of Magazine Verse and Yearbook of American Poetry* (Palm Springs: Monitor Book Co., 1988)].
    Caprice: section 5 as "Years Without News," in 2 July 1990 issue.

These poems were written over many years and have undergone many changes. I wish to thank some of the people who read them and helped me to improve them. *Mil gracias* to my friend and wise editor at *Prairie Schooner*, Hilda Raz, for always taking the time to read the work I send her; my gratitude also to the good friends who read various versions of the manuscript: Kathryn Locey, Lorraine Lopez, Hugh Ruppersburg, and especially Mark Jarman, whose keen observations helped me in the making and remaking of several of these poems. Thanks also to my wonderful research assistant, Billie Bennett, for all she does for me, and to Dory Ruderfer for the technical wizardry that made my work easier. I am deeply grateful for the support of the University of Georgia's Center for Humanities and Arts and to its director, Betty Jean Craige, for the research fellowship that allowed me time to finish this book. I also wish to thank Nicole Mitchell, director of the University of Georgia Press, for her tireless efforts to assure that poetry will continue to find a home in Georgia. Many thanks as always to my agent, Liz Darhansoff. Finally, I want to acknowledge my friend Jane Pasanen for encouraging me to do the work.

ONE

Beginning in Spanish

Beans: An Apologia for Not Loving to Cook

FOR TANYA

For me memory turns on the cloying smell of boiling beans
in a house of women waiting, waiting for wars, affairs, periods
of grieving, the rains, *el mal tiempo,* to end, the phrase
used both for inclement weather and to abbreviate the aftermath
of personal tragedies. And they waited for beans to boil.
My grandmother would put a pot on the slow fire
at dawn, and all day long, the stones she had dropped in, hard
and dry as a betrayed woman's eyes, slowly softened, scenting
the house with the essence of waiting. Beans.
I grew to hate them.
Red kidney beans whose name echoes of blood, and that are shaped
like inner organs, I hated them in their jaw-breaking rawness
and I hated them as they yielded to the fire.

The women waited in turns by the stove
rapt by the alchemy of unmaking. The mothers turned hard
at the stove, resisting our calls with the ultimate threat
of burned beans. The vigil made them statues, rivulets
of sweat coursing down their faces, pooling at their collarbones.
They turned hard away from our demands for attention and love,
their eyes and hands making sure beans would not burn
and rice would not stick, unaware of our longing
for our mothers' spirits to return back to the soft sac
that once held us, safely tucked among their inner organs,
smelling the beans they cooked for others,
through their pores.

The beans took half a child's lifetime to cook,
and when they were ready to bring to table
in soup bowls, the women called the men first
in high voices like whistles pitched above our range,
food offered like sacred, steaming sacrifice to *los hombres*.
El hambre entered the room with them, hunger
as a spectral presence, called forth from whatever other realm
the women visited when they cooked, their bodies
remaining on earth to watch the beans
while they flew away from us for hours.

                           As others fed
I watched the dog at the screen door, legs trembling,
who whimpered and waited for the scrap. I hated
the growling of pleasure when at last it got its gory bone.
I resisted the lessons of the kitchen then, fearing
the Faustian exchanges of adults, the shape-shifting nature
of women by the fire.

Now it is my daughter who keeps a voluntary vigil by the stove.
She loves the idea of cooking as chemistry, and the Tao
of making food. Her waiting for the beans to boil is a meditation
on the transformative properties of matter; a gift of memory food
from my island. And I come out of my poem to partake, to share
her delight in the art of feeding, like a recently freed captive
of a long-ago war, capable at last of a peaceful surrender
to my old nemesis, *el hambre*.

Before the Storm

We are talking in whispers
about what is worth saving. A box of photographs
is pushed under the bed, and the rendering
of Jesus knocking at somebody's door, a hesitant young man,
that arrived with us in each new house, and another
of his dear mother holding his poor broken body
not many years later, are taken down
from their precarious places on the walls.
We surprise each other with our choices.
                                  She fills boxes
while I watch the sky for signs, though I feel,
rather than see, nature is readying
for the scourge. Falling silent, the birds seek safety
in numbers, and the vagabond dogs cease their begging
for scraps. The avocados are dropping
from the laden trees in her backyard
as if by choice. Bad weather always brings in a good crop
of the water-fruit, she tells me; it is the land
offering us a last meal.
                            On the outer islands, the fragile homes
of the poor are already in its jaws, the shelters we see on film;
all those bodies huddled in the unnatural dark, the wind howling
like a hungry dog in the background, make us stand solemn.
On the mainland my family and friends will watch
the satellite pictures of this storm with trepidation
as it unravels over the Caribbean. But I am already too close
to see the whole picture. Here, there is
a saturated mantle descending,
a liquid fullness in the air, like a woman feels
before the onset of labor. Finally,

the growing urgency of the sky, and I am strangely excited,
knowing that I am as ready as I will ever be,
should I have another fifty years to go,
to go with my mother
toward higher ground. And when we come home, if
we come home, if there is a home where we believe
we left one, it will all be different.

Lessons of the Past

I was born the year my father learned to march in step
with other men, to hit bull's-eyes, to pose for sepia photos
in dress uniform outside Panamanian nightspots—pictures
he would send home to his pregnant teenage bride inscribed:
To my best girl.

       My birth
made her *La Madona*, a husbandless young woman
with a legitimate child, envied by all the tired women
of the pueblo as she strolled my carriage down dirt roads,
both of us dressed in fine clothes bought with army checks.

       When he came home,
he bore gifts: silk pajamas from the Orient for her; a pink
iron crib for me. People filled our house to welcome him.
He played Elvis loud and sang along in his new English.
She sat on his lap and laughed at everything.
They roasted a suckling pig out on the patio. Later,
no one could explain how I had climbed over the iron bars
and into the fire. Hands lifted me up quickly, but not before
the tongues had licked my curls.

       There is a picture of me
taken soon after: my hair clipped close to my head,
my eyes enormous—about to overflow with fear.
I look like a miniature of one of those women
in Paris after World War II, hair shorn,
being paraded down the streets in shame,
for having loved the enemy.

But then things changed,
and some nights he did not come home. I remember
hearing her cry in the kitchen. I sat on the rocking chair
waiting for my cocoa, learning how to count, *uno, dos, tres,*
cuatro, cinco, on my toes. So that when he came in,
smelling strong and sweet as sugarcane syrup,
I could surprise my *papasito*—
who liked his girls smart, who did not like crybabies—
with a new lesson, learned well.

A Theory of Chaos: October 1962

Each moment is the fruit of forty thousand years. The minute-winning days,
like flies, buzz home to death, and every moment is a window on all time.
THOMAS WOLFE

I was just ten, and far away
from all I had known, when I was sent
to find help for my sick mother.
Ships and warplanes
were gathering around Cuba
and my father was in one of them,
silenced by national security,
dead or alive, we did not know.
I could not speak English
and so was totally alone.
Words in the new language
were simmering in my head
like bees trying to communicate
salvation through dance.
My life was chaos
shaped by chance, biology,
and either *el destino*
or circumstance. I did not know
or care then
that I carried the coded message
to make language from pure need.

But then,
as I entered the too-bright drugstore—
alien as a spaceship, sudden
as Ezekiel's wheel,
mysterious as the Annunciation—
I could understand the speech of people,

I could read the labels,
and I raised my head up
to hear the voice
over the loudspeaker.
All was clear,
and fell into place,
even the blinding light.

It had taken ten minutes
of absolute dread, of nearly drowning
in my own chemicals,

and maybe of synapses folding
into dams and bridges: a million butterflies
lifting their minuscule wings as one,
gale winds over Iceland.
And the strange attractor this time
dressed in aqua and pink robes,
and feathers, called down by my mother
from fevered dreams of Guardian Angels
to aid me.

Given the gift of tongues,
my heart and brain
synchronized their wing-beats,
or cranked a secret engine
just long enough to allow
one small, frightened girl to fly
a little, to hover low over the chaos,
and just above where meaning begins.

Dominoes: A Meditation on the Game

The first record of them comes from twelfth-century China, where they were used for divination rather than gaming. Dominoes are usually made of ivory, consisting of twenty-eight rectangular tiles. Each tile is bisected, and the halves that are not blank bear dots numbering one to six, representing all possible number combinations, ranging from double blank to double six. In their Western incarnation, dominoes have tended to be far more popular as a game than as a tool for divination. Certain tiles are thought to be lucky for the player, regardless of the outcome of the game.

Cee

Domino games may go on for years and through generations. There are Cuban men in Calle Ocho who have been playing since the Revolution. They have taught their sons and their grandsons to play. There is no end to these domino games. The men play in waves, rising only when the new players come in at sunset, taking up the game the next day. They sit before their rows of black-and-white tiles, twenty-eight in all, arranged like the headstones of dead soldiers. Twenty-eight in all, each tile is bisected, and the halves that are not blank bear dots numbering one to six, representing all possible number combinations, ranging from double blank to double six. Certain tiles are thought to be lucky for the player, regardless of the outcome of the game.

Cee

On January 8, 1959, Fidel Castro led his ragged army into Havana. The previous night Don Miguel had called a game early after having drawn a double blank under the roof of his own home. In the city, his son Miguelito had drawn a double six and spent the night drunk on his own luck. Don Miguelito plays all day on Calle Ocho. He has taught his son and grandson to play. In their Western incarnation, dominoes have tended to be far more popular as a game than as a tool for divination. Certain tiles are thought to be lucky for the player, regardless of the outcome of the game.

Cee

In '62, my father, called to duty at sea, left his game in Puerto Rico forever, and learned that *embargo* is an American word. *Sin embargo,* he had also drawn a double six in his last hand. Aboard his ship, there were no domino games. No one played. He later said the ivory pieces in a cigar box under his bunk clicked like the bones of the dead all that long October month, when the water between the islands got rough. I can still see him studying the black-and-white faces, twenty-eight in all, representing all possible number combinations, ranging from double blank to double six. I never saw him play again. My father's bones lie under a headstone listing all the wars since his last game. He did not lose his life in a war, but he lost his love of the game. My father's ivory tiles, twenty-eight in all, feel like dry bones in my hands. I cannot play. It is lately that I learn that six-six is the luckiest domino of them all, predicting happiness, success, and prosperity, while the direst of omens is a double blank with danger, despair, and death all to be written in black ink on an ivory page. This is an old game. The first record of dominoes comes from twelfth-century China, where they were used for divination. In their Western incarnation, dominoes have tended to be far more popular as a game. Certain tiles are thought to be lucky for the player, regardless of the outcome of the game.

Information on the history of dominoes was found in *Mysteries of the Unknown,* by the Editors of Time-Life Books (New York: Time-Life Books, 1988).

from A Sailor's Wife's Journal

But I waste my heart away longing for Odysseus.
BOOK 19, *THE ODYSSEY*

1.

Dear Odysseus:
The moon looms over our house, its face split
in mockery of my grief. I have
seen it change expressions six times
since you left. Half a year ago
you last made love to me
on the lap of this old tree you carved
into our marriage bed. The branches
you said were the fingers of gods
blessing our union seem now to threaten;
their shadows fall across my body
one by one with the movement of the moon.

                  Before your journey
you took me to your ship. Together we watched
your men raise the sails. Flapping in the good wind,
they were the wings of a great white bird
you held captive to move your ship with its desire
for flight. To the sounds of its struggle
we came together in your cabin. In the dimness
of this man-place, you promised me with a thousand kisses
that you would return, Odysseus.

                  A sudden gust
has swollen the canopy of our bed
like the sails of a ship. *My* ship, Odysseus,
a ship that goes nowhere.

2.

Dear Odysseus:
This morning a lark entered my chamber
alighting on the lowest branch of a tree
that is our marriage bed. He sang for me.
At daybreak, I heard chanting and laughter
in the distance. It was a crowd of young worshippers
welcoming spring, walking home
from the fields they had blessed with wine,
songs, and lovemaking. The girls walked arm-in-arm
ahead of the young men whose eyes were fixed
on their graceful bodies like mariners
first sighting land.

                      When you came for me,
we walked on my father's fields, and you said
green was not the color of your destiny. The sea
was calling you even then. Birdsong and nursing calf
amused but did not hold you, the mystery
of earth-grown things, the passing
of Apollo's chariot were matters for the minds
of lesser men, you said.

                    Stars enticed you
for their coded messages, Odysseus; the moon
was a torch held over the chart of the night sky,
so you, forever captain, could plot
your next destination.

                  I have begun to see things
more clearly, as if my eyes were stronger
from willing your ship to appear on the horizon.
On the ledge of a window facing the setting sun,
I found a moth with nearly invisible wings
I wished into flight. I watched a leaf
leap down from the branch of a tall tree
to ride the gathering wind.

I wait for clouds,
moving slowly as wounded soldiers, to bring me
the smell of rain—a distant promise I take in
in deep breaths.

3.

Today I followed my servant, Hestia, down the dusty path
that leads away from the sea. As I trudged toward
the barren hills that separate my house from her world,
her stiff back told me
that a woman walking home after a day of laboring
over someone else's hearth
had nothing to share with a fortunate fool
strolling in the heat of late afternoon
for pleasure.
                    As we approached the last clump of trees
huddled together like beggars at the edge of the village,
I gave up the contest of wills. I followed Hestia's brown form
with my eyes, as she descended into a marketplace
filled with hagglers, stray dogs, and flies—until
she became part of the crowd.

    I stood there with my arms around a thin old tree
for a long time, listening to the sounds of words
I could not decipher, the empty cadences of far-away voices
rising and falling.
                    Without you, Odysseus,
I have come to hate living on this island—the constant whine
of the sea licking its own wounds. If I could, I would follow
the vagrant gulls to crowded places and feast on crumbs.
I would wait with the winning patience of birds
for someone to extend an open hand.

4.

LINES FOR THE DROWNED SAILOR WASHED ASHORE

When I first saw you break through
the wine-dark waters, your body
blocked the setting sun, an aureole
of light—transforming you into a god.
               The tide rocked you,
spread your yellow hair crowned with seaweed,
opened and closed your limp hands—filling you,
emptying you, like a mother gone mad with grief
working over a dead child.
               I stood at the edge of the sea
until the sounds of the retreating waves,
like the suckling of an infant at the breast,
or of a man loving a woman's body, became one
with the rhythm of my breathing.
               Tonight you will travel
to Lord Poseidon's realm, down to that silent place
where there is no memory or desire,
only the slow melting away of the flesh.

5.

Everyone treats me like a widow. Our son weeps alone
in his chamber, his eyes frightened like those of a fawn
abandoned in the forest. Servants whisper in the hallways.
                                        Thick currents
of sea-smells drift in through the windows of these rooms,
labyrinth of my sleepless nights. I sit very still listening
to our poet tune his lyre in the garden below. As the sun sets,
he will turn his eyes to our island's rocky shore.
                                        In the deepening pool
of nightfall, I chant a spell against sorrow, and brace myself,
knowing that in a moment of weakness my soul can be stolen
by a jealous god and dragged across the sky
like someone's wish.

Look at the sky for directions, Husband, but *never*
speak longingly of me.

Siempre

Tomorrow I will be with my mother
in a different world, only three hours'
flight time away, yet foreign as Venus.
Tomorrow I will be facing the mirror
that reflects my future. Soon
I will feel a need
to step into it, growing smaller
to fit into her tiny kingdom
of two-by-four-inch memories.
She, whose beauty she can now recall
as her fondest memory, she and I
will turn the pages of the family album,
and gradually I will become
a child again. Again, I will follow
her laughter through the unfamiliar
apartments and houses in new cities
she now calls *sitios*, empty places
she had to transform into homes.

She, whose nervous energy was a presence
I felt hovering near me like a phantom sibling
even when she left the room.
She, who is still vibrant with her other selves:
the timidly exultant teenage bride, the anxiety-driven
young mother in a strange country, and always
the battle to keep loving life in spite of exile,
loneliness, and the early death
of her husband's spirit. She and I
will turn the pages of the album together.
All is perfectly preserved: the posed smiles,
the Sunday clothes, the handsome man at attention

next to his pretty wife, the radiance
of his crisp Navy uniform, and me,
reflective in my communion dress.

I can count on this: All is always well
in the past. *Siempre.*

Tomorrow I will be with my mother,
but today I remember my father.
My father gone so long
he is now a decade younger than I.
My father of the luminous brown eyes
trained to see in the dark, scanning the horizon
for signs of storm, who brought his despair to us
along with gifts: dolls dressed in the costumes
of countries he took no pleasure in exploring,
silk from far-off places where he practiced
his *soledad,* his *tristeza*: Madrid, Palermo,
Pompeii, Tripoli, Guantanamo Bay.

Father of the vigilant gaze,
forever expecting to be called away.
Father of elegant sadness.
Father of the crisp white *guayaberas*
and the razor's-edge-creased pants,
of the military-issue black-as-coffins shoes,
shined every morning before coffee.
Father of darkness.
Father of pain without end.
Father, today I remember
the terrible beauty of your yearning;
I carry it with me *siempre,*
the gift you did not intend to give me.

The Poet's Work

Inside this old movie house still open for retrospectives,
I first savored the cool dark knowing of not having to watch
a film half as interesting as my life. My first kiss, last row,
Saturday matinee. That parking lot across the street was once
a playground for the dust-and-sweaty summer children
of the city. At fourteen, two on a swing
after a sudden August downpour emptied the lot,
an inspiration of long slender legs locked together in perfect synchrony:
the dizzying motion, rush of blood, desire etching its name
into bone. I knew nothing like this would ever happen again
in Paris or in Rome. Church bells, how right the metaphor,
church bells sent me running home, wet skirt clinging
to my body like newfound faith, blood rising
toward a Pentecost. I knew I had to write the poem.
I don't remember his name. His name did not matter even then.
I was working on the poem.

Here Is a Picture of Me

Balancing myself, hands on hips,
feet lined one after the other
on a cement wall between city buildings,
in the background a broken fire escape
I used as a swing, as a trapeze.
I am skinny and brash, thirteen or fourteen,
aware of my bones, of the angles and curves
reforming my skin. I am challenging gravity
in my tight checked capri pants
and man's shirt tied at the waist, pulled taut
over the one eighth of an inch padded points
waiting to fulfill their promise.
What was I thinking while I posed
for my neighbor's new Polaroid camera?
My parents are outside the frame, waiting
to see if the present moment can really
be captured on film. In seconds,
my mother will exclaim *¡Oye!*
and *¡Mira!* as I emerge from a milky bluish sea
spilling into the black square she holds
open-palmed, taller and older
than she remembers me only sixty seconds ago.
Father will look away as if he has suddenly heard
something in the distance,
perhaps a fire alarm.

That Old Tune

In her siesta-dimmed bedroom, my mother is singing
along with a recording of Daniel Santos, *La Voz*,
the drug-martyred, woman-haunted Puerto Rican soul
made suffering flesh. I hear them moaning over a woman
who was the needle in the compass of his life; his passion for her
like the treacherous currents of a once tranquil river, its undertow
now pulling him down to his death. In the refrain, he curses
the bed they had slept on—it has turned to stone,
De piedra ha de ser mi cama.

I can hear them from my room, the noon sun
pressing down on the wall. *De piedra la cabecera.* I am lying
very still under a cool sheet. A beetle circles over the bed, whirring
its wings at a mad pace, trying to lift
its heavy body with its ponderous abdomen away
from the threat of so much white space. I direct my breath
toward him—letting him almost free—then pulling
him down to where his frantic drone almost drowns
the voices coming from her room. I imagine her
lying on her back, her eyes open but unseeing,
her hands crossed over her chest, imitating
the corpse of her husband—the formal stranger
in dress uniform we have just viewed in the funeral home.

In her darkened room, my mother sings along
with Daniel Santos, who is dying of passion for a woman
who is the needle on a compass always pointing south,
on a scratched record; in a vein taking the poison of her love
to his tormented heart, the voice
rising from deep within a ravaged body—kept alive
solely on yearning. *La mujer que a mí me quiera.*

I can hear that old tune now. Its sad and erotic melody. Its refrain of ecstasy and pain. *La mujer que a mí me quiera, ha de quererme de veras.* I would recognize it anywhere.

First Job: The Southern Sweets Sandwich Shop and Bakery

Lillie Mae glows, she hates the word sweat,
as she balances a platter of baked sweets over her head,
showing me how to walk with grace
even under the weight of minimum wage
and a mountain of cookies,
turnovers, and tarts, which she blames
for her "voluptuous" figure. She calls me
"shuggah," and is teaching me the job.
We are both employed by Mr. Raymond, who keeps her
in a little house outside of town.

I'm fifteen, living my first year
in the strange country called Georgia.
Lillie Mae hired me for my long black hair
she couldn't wait to braid, and for my gift
of tongues, which she witnessed as I turned
my mother's desire for a sugar bubble
she called a merengue into something nearly equal
behind the glass wall.
"Shuggah," she will on occasion call me
out front, "talk foreign for my friend."
And I will say whatever comes into my head,
"You're a pig, Mr. Jones, I see your hand
under the table stroking her thigh." If they're impressed
with my verbal prowess, I may suggest something tasty
from our menu; if they presume I am Pocahontas
at the palace, there only to amuse their royal selves,
I tell them, smiling sweetly, to try the mierda,
which is especially good that day. Soon I can make
anything sound appetizing in Spanish.

Lillie Mae carries her silver-plated tray
to Mr. Raymond for inspection, looking seductive
as a plump Salomé in her fitted white nylon uniform.

He is a rotund King Herod asking for the divinity
though he knows it is on its way. She sorts her delicacies,
pointing out the sugar-coated wedding cookies with the tips
of her pink glue-on nails she is so proud of.

"Because, Shuggah, a woman's hands should always
be soft and beautiful; never mind you scrubbed, waxed
pushed, pulled, and carried all blessed day.
That's what a man expects."

I watch them as they talk shop and lock eyes,
but cannot quite imagine the carnival of their couplings.
Instead, I see them licking their chops over strudel,
consuming passion while ensconced in her edible house
with peppermint stick columns and gingerbread walls.

In the kitchen of the Southern Sweets the black cook,
Margaret, worships at the altar of her Zenith radio. Hank Aaron
is working his way to heaven. She is bone-sticking thin,
despises sweets, loves only her man Hank, Otis Redding,
and a smoke. She winks at me when he connects,
dares to ignore Mr. Raymond when Aaron is up. Mysteriously
the boss-man understands the priority of home runs,
and the sacrilege of speaking ordinary words like my
"triple decker club on a bun with fries" frozen at tongue-tip
when Margaret holds up one bony finger at us, demanding
a little respect for the man at the plate.

That windowless kitchen, with its soul-melting
hot floors and greasy walls, had to disappear for her,
like a magician's trick at the sweet snap of the ball and bat
that sent her into orbit, her eyes rolling back in ecstasy,
mouth circling the O in wonder as if she had seen the glory.

At closing, Lillie Mae fluffs her boot-black curls,
heads home to entertain her sugar daddy or to be alone,
glue on new nails, pin-curl her hair, and practice walking
gracefully under heavy trays.

I have homework to do, words to add to my arsenal
of sweet-sounding missiles for mañana.
My father waits for me in his old brown Galaxy.
He is wary of these slow-talking tall Southerners, another race

he must avoid or face; tired of navigating his life,
which is a highway crowded with strangers sealed in their vehicles,
and badly marked with signs that he will never fully understand.
I offer him a day-old doughnut, but no, at least from me
he does not have to accept second-best anything.

We drive by the back lot, where Margaret stands
puffing small perfect clouds, her eyes fixed to a piece of sky
between the twin smokestacks of Continental Can, and beyond
what I can see from where I am. Still tracking Aaron's message
hovering above us all in the airwaves?
Her lips move and I can read the drawled-out "shee-it"
followed by that characteristic shake of her head
that meant, Girl, in this old world,
some things are still possible.

Notes for My Daughter Studying Math
on the Morning of a New Year

Mira, mira, our Spanish-speaking kin
are always saying. Look and look again. It amuses us,
this insistence on seeing, even when they mean listen.
Could it be that they keep the world less at bay
than we their exiled children? That they can see
emotions in color? Anger is the scarlet
hibiscus, joy, the blue of the Puerto Rican sky
after a July rainstorm, and grief,
a black mantilla on the head of the woman
sitting alone in the last pew of an empty church.
Mira, Hija, I say to you in my mother's voice,
when I mean listen, and you may turn your eyes
in the direction of some unexpected bit of wonder:
the dull gray city pigeon is iridescent
in a certain slant of light, and she perches
at *your* window. If this is not enough, *pues, mira,*
the sun shines indiscriminately over everything. *Mira, Hija.*
Even the shadows make interesting designs on the concrete.

Listen: whatever the weather, when you step outside
and breathe deeply, you inhale the history
of our race in each molecule: Eve's desire,
Cleopatra's ambition, Magdalene's guilt,
the New World of Isabel of Castile,
the fierce conquests of Elizabeth, and the genius
of Sor Juana and Virginia Woolf; here too remains
the labored breath of an old woman

fishing a day's meal at the Dumpster,
and the fears of the fourteen-year-old runaway
who will soon run out of breath; my own relief
as the nurse settled you in my arms
on the day you arrived
into the breathless world.

Try to speak
in Spanish in your dreams. Say *sol,*
día, sueños, as you fall asleep. See
if you can believe that tomorrow may be the day
you have been designing in the dark,
an algebra from particles of light
swirling behind your eyelids—
your own private theory of relativity.

Where You Need to Go

My life began here in this pueblo
now straining against its boundaries
and still confused about its identity:
Spanish village or tourist rest stop?
with its centuries-old church
where on Sundays pilgrims on their knees
beg a dark Madonna for a miracle,
then have lunch at Burger King.

Here is the place
where I first wailed for life
in a pre-language understood by all
in the woman-house where I was born,
where absent men in military uniform
paraded on walls alongside calendars
and crosses, and telegrams were delivered
by frightened adolescent boys
who believed all coded words from Korea
were about death. But sometimes
they were just a *"Bueno, Mujer,"*
to the women who carried on
their blood duties on the home front.

I know this place,
although I have been away most of my life.
I have never really recovered
from my plunge, that balmy February day,
into the unsteady hands
of the nearly blind midwife,
as she mumbled prayers in Latin
to the Holy Mother, who had herself
been spared the anguish

this old woman witnessed year after year,
to the aroma of herbal teas
brewed for power in *la lucha,* and the haunting
of the strangely manic music
that accompanies both beginnings
and endings on this island. I absorbed it all
through my pores. And it remains
with me still, as a vague urge
to reconnect.

Today, opening my eyes again
in my mother's house,
I know I will experience certain things
that come to me in dreams and in déjà vu:
the timeless tolling of bells,
because time must be marked for mortal days
in minutes, in hours, and in measured intervals,
to remind us as we drink our morning *café*
that we too shall turn to dust; the rustling
of palm fronds against venetian blinds, of water
running over a woman's hands,
pots and pans put in their places, living sounds
from my childhood; and muffled words
I cannot quite decipher, spoken in a language
I now have to translate, like signs
in a foreign airport you recognize
as universal symbols, and soon
their true meaning will come to you. It must.
For this is the place where you decide
where you need to go.

TWO

El Amor, el Azul, a Hibiscus

I love

the wild herons who return each year to the marshy outskirts.

What I invaded has

invaded me.

DENISE LEVERTOV, "WAYS OF CONQUEST"

Rice: An Ars Poetica

Her calling is to carve all the truth
she finds on single grains of rice. She spends her days
gleaning through piles of Grade A long grain
Mahatma, butterflying fingers feeling
for the perfect one, pearly as a baby's tooth, a planed
oval on which she will script with a nearly invisible
needle in vertical lines,
like Buddhist text:
> The Preamble to the Constitution
> The chorus of John Lennon's "Revolution"
> The Collected Dickinson
> The First Amendment

She is now working on fitting the Lord's Prayer
upon the face of a single grain, but has failed
beyond "deliver us from evil."
She will attempt it again
on an anomalous grain she found
nearly three times larger
than nature usually allows. She vows
to persevere until the kingdom, until the power
and the glory, until the amen.
Her dream is to buy a silo full of rice
from all over the world,
to dive into the dry sea of plenty,
and to find that perfect grain,
blank as the future, where she will preserve:

Don Quixote's windmill scene,
also, on his first seeing Dulcinea
"Ode on a Grecian Urn"
Aretha Franklin's "Respect"
Parts of *To the Lighthouse*
Some of the Psalms
All of the Song of Solomon
"Satisfaction" by the Rolling Stones.

The Superstition Poems

THE GIFT OF A KNIFE

When I was very young,
she let me shower with her once,
and I saw it, the scar that divided her body
in half like a sardonic smile. Eye level
to me, it was a preface to my life
as a woman. When will I have one?
I asked her, imagining the silver knife
that had exposed the mystery
of my mother's body, opening a door
for her children; she had survived
the good agony of birth, payment for the gift
of a baby in your arms. It was not an entrance,
she said, but an exit, *la operación,* given her
for free at eighteen, a gift from the government,
to make sure she did not let any more
babies enter a small island already crowded
as the stall we were in, the cubicle
where I was having trouble breathing
through the steam, hearing her words, *no más hijos,*
through the water. I felt our bodies were separated
by oceans. And my mother's wound—those pale hieroglyphs
over a crescent—it was the writing on the wall
of a dead queen's tomb, a message
in an ancient language
I had yet to decipher.

THE PLEASURES OF FEAR

We played a hiding game,
the son of my mother's friend and I,
until he chased me into the toolshed
and bolted the door from outside. It was there,
in the secret, moist dark, the child's game changed
to adventure. As I listened through the splintered wood
to his ragged breath, his weight pressing down
on the thin wood, making it groan, waiting
while I stood on the other side, I was
caught in time, thrilled and frightened by his power,
by his power to strike, and mine to yield.

I crouched close to the ground
inhaling the sour-sweet potpourri of rancid oil,
rotting wood, old leather, and rust. I could have died
right then and there, of anticipation,
and become one with the molecules
in the laden air. I was deliciously afraid of all
the invisible creeping, crawling dangers inhabiting
the luscious ground where I squatted to pee,
allowing impulse and need to fully overtake me,
inviting all the demons that reside in dark damp
hiding places into my most secret self.

Not since then has pleasure and fear in the dark
been so finely tuned in my mind, except perhaps
in moments of passion when all we know
is surrendered to the demands of skin and blood.

Then the pizzicato of the predictable afternoon shower
on that half remembered island, rain every day at four,
and her piercing voice, growing nearer,
the cutting slash of light. She had caught the boy
peeking through a crack at me doing what?
She did not want to know.

I was sent straight to the bath, as if
the delectable stink of danger I had discovered
could ever be washed off with plain soap and water.

THE LESSON OF THE TONGUE

A month of rainstorms in the afternoon, and in the kitchen
the women are balancing the weight of their crosses. The girl listens
to them complain about the neighbor's son, who has been sent home
from the jungle, still wearing camouflage, and wounded
in some way they will not say aloud.

A sudden burst of thunder
propels their Spanish toward the heavens: *¡Santa Bárbara bendita!*
At a command from her mother, she drops her *World History II*—cover
for her eavesdropping of revelations in the mother tongue—and runs
to shut the windows in the apartment down the hall, since *he*,
thorn-in-his-mother's-flesh, won't care
if it is fire or flood.

He lies
on his mother's flowered sofa
as if it were a fresh grave, reading *Action* comics all day,
ignoring her incessant pleas to rise, to work,
to do something with his life *¡Por Dios!* Invisible to her eyes,
not yet adjusted to the dark, the girl cannot see the man
lying immobile as a corpse, who will bring her down
with a sweep of his arm—a scythe felling her in one motion.
The scream begins to rise in her throat—
but he demands silence, one finger crossed over his lips—
promising to share a secret. She is frozen like small prey
caught by the commanding eye
of eagle or owl.

She is almost lost
within the circles, the bull's-eye, his tongue describes,
coming ever closer to the location of her heart. Her body
is poised for flight, like a marble at thumb's tip.

Then he opens his eyes,
and the yellow fire she sees raging deep within wakes her
from the dream. She runs back to the women,
now whispering by candlelight, or praying
for the lifting of the dark. Alarmed by her wild look,
they demand she tell them what is wrong. *¿Qué pasa?*
But she cannot say.
She cannot say.
For she has swallowed her tongue.

She was the woman with no name. The blank filled in
with *La Fulana* when children were around
and to avoid the curse of naming evil.
But we knew her—she was the wild girl
we were not allowed to play with,
who painted her face with her absent mother's makeup
and who always wanted to be *wife*
when we played house. She was bored
with other games, preferred to turn the radio loud
to songs about women and men
loving and fighting to guitar, *maracas,* and drums.
She wanted to be a dancer on the stage,
dressed in nothing but yellow feathers.

And she would grow up careless as a bird,
losing contact with her name in the years
when her body was light enough to fly.
By the time gravity began to pull her down
to where the land animals chewed the cud
of domestic routine, she was a different
species. She had become *La Fulana,* the creature
bearing the jagged scars of wings on her back,
whose name should not be mentioned
in the presence of impressionable little girls
who might begin to wonder about flight,
how the houses of their earth-bound mothers,
the fields and the rivers, and the schools and the churches
would look from above.

BLACK SILK SHIRT

He tries it on
on impulse. It is tapered
in the shape of his dark self,
his sleek doppelgänger,
and it feels like the long hair
of the woman he has conjured
into his dreams,
of lying under a black starless sky,
where he breathed the pitch of night.

No, he thinks, I will not
wear this, beginning to let go
of the whim. Then the sudden
presence of the Puerto Rican salesgirl
who runs her red-lacquered nails,
without pressure, down the seam
from shoulder to wrist, the way
she says ¡Que bello! seals him
inside the silk, which settles
over his frame like grafted skin.
In the ebony talisman
suspended between her breasts,
he sees himself scaling eternity.
And the yes escapes his mouth
even before she asks,
"Do you want it?"

Although he has been away too long this time, and a foreign smell may still be clinging to him—he knows she is sensitive to this—she lets him in, draws a warm bath scented with Verbena, Bloodroot, and Rue; herbs from the thriving garden she tends in a small plot outside her kitchen. He likes hearing her say their names in her own tongue, and she does so as she pours the water over him like a blessing: *Azafrán, Enebro, Mandrágora, and Nenúfar.* Afterwards, she anoints his whole body with oil, offers to cut his hair grown long and wild—he can't refuse the lure of her knowing hands—the blade's run on the back of his neck sending shivers through him as in sex—making them both laugh aloud. Kneeling, she takes his traveling feet into her hands, trims his hard-as-horn toenails— silver scissors cool against his skin. She kisses the tender spot between his ankle and heel. He feels the gentle pressure of her teeth and thinks of shells he has stepped on at the beach—strange how vulnerable he feels with her kneeling at his feet. He has to smile, watching her gather up each strand of hair and nail clipping from the floor. She wraps the commas and little crescent moons like gifts in scraps of paper he recognizes as lines torn from a poem or prayer, before placing them over a candle's small flame. For a moment, he is alarmed by the smell of singed flesh, but as she slips into their bed, folding herself perfectly into his body's curve, he breathes in only the familiar jasmine on her skin, a scent she mixes herself just to please him. *Such a peculiar woman,* he thinks. But he is an understanding man, and she loves him like no other. He is too tired for lovemaking just then, and of course, she understands. He soon surrenders to a deep and easy sleep, cradled in the fragrant arms of a good woman.

OLD WOMEN IN THEIR ROOMS

. . . little packages, oh yes,
all old women make little packages
and stow them under their beds.

FROM *THE OBSCENE BIRD OF NIGHT*
A NOVEL BY JOSÉ DONOSO

Stored under groaning mattresses
are the remnants of lives
wrapped in little packages, taped
or tied with string: photos
jaundiced with age, of couples
standing stiff as corpses
at the greatest distance the frame
will allow, of taciturn infants
held by women in breast-flattening
black crepe and satin frocks
buttoned to their chins; stacks
of magazines; moth-balled bags
of men's shirts—dead husbands'
Sunday best, *ropa de muertos,* becoming
one moist lump; balls of string
solid as tumors; baby clothes, cracked,
yellowed frayed lace, *trajes de bautismo;*
and old shoes curling tongue-to-heel.
All of it now homogenized, velvety
to the touch.

In the thick air
of wet coughs and medicinal tea,
everything returns to what it once was:
paper to pulp,
cloth to fiber,
dust to dust.

THE CRUEL SEASON

It is the light at the center of every cell.
It is what sent the snake coiling and flowing forward
happily all spring through the green leaves before
he came to the road.
MARY OLIVER

This thawing earth,
down with a fever
that will break in beauty,
like a Victorian woman
dying in childbirth,
translucent flesh ablaze,
eyes brilliant, craving
release; deep in her agony,
eager for the red dance
to begin.

These jonquils that will push stems
through late frost. Obscene
yellow, bulbous,
sepals tinged with ochre,
leaves limp from the struggle—sad
as the drunken girl you remember
from the senior dance: yellow hair,
green chiffon gown, spread
like a stain on the white tiles
of the bathroom floor.

Old, rusty nails
will rise like gasps
out of floorboards in old houses,
released by sun shrinking
the lumber, startling old people

in their sleep—a rehearsal
in a darkened theater.
Wood will dissolve
deep in rain-heavy earth,
pedicels dig like grave robbers,
seeking red, and roots—blind, parasitic
worms—coil around cartilage
and bone—picking everything clean.
Soon enough, corollas will beg open
everywhere, like the beaks
of ravenous baby birds,
and it will be spring.

ALMS OUTSIDE THE PACKAGE STORE, PEACHTREE STREET

I am sitting in a parked car, waiting for my friend
who will take her time picking out a wine
to celebrate success and our reunion,

when a pile of rags next to a Dumpster stands up,
a face right out of El Greco, one
of his fools from Toledo,

who approaches my window with his hand held out,
who comes so close that his breath makes a ring
like a kiss on the glass separating us.

He is toothless as a newborn baby.
I know what he wants, only money. He says
nothing, but he turns up his palms

to show me—what?—that he is poor? unarmed?
also made of flesh? But a new set of headlights
spirits him away:

he of the black coat shiny with wear,
of the comical ears and the innocent smile,
of the painful limping off

to another non-encounter. On the long drive home,
the bottle I hold to my chest feels heavy and cold.
"Too expensive," I have said of the wine,
which bubbles like anger or remorse at every turn.

A flower native to the tropics, the hibiscus prefers the direct light of the sun. Its petals form a large trumpet-shaped corolla. Protruding from the corolla is a stamen tube with female stigmas at the tip. The petals are smooth, but the leaves of the hibiscus are coarsely serrated. The flowers of some species of hibiscus can be used to clean and shine black shoes. The flower lasts only a day; at night, each corolla folds its petals tightly around the stamen and drops to the ground.

I give you the hibiscus. It is a tropical flower. It prefers the direct light of the sun. The petals of each flower form a large trumpet-shaped corolla. A musical instrument. *Protruding from the corolla is a stamen tube with female stigmas at the tip.* A mouth. A tongue. Bring it to your lips. *Its petals are smooth.* The trumpet's notes will be a siren's song; low, melodious, and commanding. Bring it to your lips, play it. It will feel like a kiss. Beware the leaves. *The leaves of the hibiscus are coarsely serrated.*

The hibiscus is a useful flower. *The flowers of some species can be used to clean and shine black shoes.* You can crush the flower; use it to shine your black shoes. It may leave a bloodlike stain on skin. A stigma. A sign. Beware the leaves. The swords, the knives. Protect your skin.

I give you the hibiscus, an ephemeral flower. It lasts only a day. At night, each corolla folds its petals tightly around the stamen and drops to the ground. A shrouded female form. A beauty in her time? Lost gospel in a scroll, too small to read.

Information found in the pamphlet *Flores de Puerto Rico y exóticas* by Edwin Miner Solá.

The tiny brown girl in Toys. The dirty pink sneakers she wears. The boxed brown Barbie she holds. The angry woman rushing up center aisle screaming "No!" The frown she wears, forehead split, the hatchet-halves of fury. The clerk walking through the mirrored wall. The angry woman yelling "No!" The clerk, "Hey, you. Stop!" Deny a child a toy. The tiny brown girl grasping boxed doll, face frozen into mask of wild resolve, tearing at plastic bubble. Hispanic Barbie smiling and smiling within, stunning in hot pink, off-the-shoulder Mexican peasant blouse and frilly rickrack-trimmed black skirt, matching black and fuchsia shoes and purse. Little brown girl in dirty pink sneakers attacking impenetrable package, using fingers and nails, mouth and teeth. Now a wild thing. Tiny brown girl quivering, mouth shaping without sound syllables we all know. *Ma-ma,* she mouths. We, standing near end of Toys. Deny a child a toy. The woman-in-a-rage cutting through, screaming "No!" Clerk in executioner stance, arm-slicing air. Pointing.

"Hey. You. Stop!" Tiny brown girl letting go of Hispanic Barbie with accessories in her clear, plastic bubble, letting go. Little brown girl begins letting go. Letting go. Letting go. Mouth opening in anguish, in loss, a cry to stop time. We, bored bargain-hunters, late-in-the-season shoppers, it stops time for us. Deny a child a toy. Hispanic Barbie falling on the shiny tile floor. We at Toys stare. Girl going limp as if bones had dissolved, sinking into shame. Letting go. Pool of shame at her feet. Hispanic Barbie, in impermeable plastic dome, middle of it all, safe from the storm, smiling and smiling, dressed to kill in hot pink off-the-shoulder top, frilly rickrack-trimmed black skirt, matching accessories. Clerk, pointing, arm a sword. Woman wearing anger, body plunged through shattered windshield, cutting through silent crowd. Grabbing child. Pool of shame. Dirty, wet, broken doll. Doll-mouth now open, now closed in consonant and one vowel, consonant and one vowel: *Ma-ma.* Sounds beginning and ending the world. Little brown girl screaming, again and again. We, near end of Toys. We look away: packaged choices in racks, long checkout lines, shiny black and white tiles.

Hispanic Barbie safe in impermeable bubble. Puddle of shame. We, standing in Toys. Little brown girl carried away in terrible embrace. Deny a child a toy.

BED-MAKING IN A FOREIGN COUNTRY

Sunday's chambermaid comes in love-sleepy
from the bed of her Juan or her José.
Smelling like caramel, like warm flan,
smiling not at me, she tucks in the rumpled
one half of the bed I have just left,
leaves the sheets taut enough for me
to use as blank pages
if I cared to write her life
in straight lines on that crisp linen.

If I offer to change places, to give her my books,
my traveling bags, and my plane ticket
to a more temperate zone, in trade for her cold-water flat
and the look in her eyes, she would shake her head no,
continuing her work, for it is an evil omen
to leave a bed unmade—it will cause
a sleepless night,
or at least the interruption of dreams
for one of us.

FOUND POEM: CHARM FOR THE LOVE OF A WOMAN

*Image magic has been practiced in every part of the world and in all periods
of history. . . . A recent example is the discovery . . . of the figure of a naked
woman, six inches long and made of modeling clay. . . . It was stuck through the
heart with a sharp sliver of hawthorn and near it were a black candle and a
sheep's heart. . . . This image may have been meant either to kill or to seduce.*
RICHARD CAVENDISH, *THE BLACK ARTS*

Shape your loved one in soft wax,
with the sex organs emphasized.
Her features too should be sharp and clear.
Across the breasts carve out her name.
Write to whom she should belong
across the back, between the shoulder blades.
Speak these words as if they were a prayer:
"May _____(insert her name) burn
with a mighty passion
only for me. May I be the reason
for every breath she takes."
Bury the figure for one day and one night
in a path you know she will take.
Dig it out with care so the limbs
will not break. Wash it three times in water,
invoking the names of God's warriors,
Michael, Raphael, and Gabriel.
Dip it in your urine or blood, let it dry.
Then pierce the heart with a new needle.

Be aware that you may need
to remake her likeness, especially the heart,
often, and to pierce it every day,
before the charm for a woman's love
will have its desired effect.

SAINT, HAIR, WATER

I surprised myself in a gallery once—
having been programmed for life
in a Catholic reverence for holy men—
with a little spasm of desire:

St. John

as in most renditions, hirsute,
hard-bodied, and intense; Christ's cousin
as my ideal lover, obsessed,
his dark eyes focused on the infinite
even as Salome danced her fatal seduction.

I wanted to step into that river
where he waited, pull him down
with me into the current, comb his skin
with my fingernails,
and make him forget
the other purpose of water.

THE ART OF SCRYING: A POEM FOR MY BIRTHDAY

In the form of divination known as scrying, a practitioner presumes to plumb the depths of hidden knowledge by concentrating on a smooth, clear, or reflective surface.

As a child of ten, I was often caught by my reflection on a smooth, clear, or reflective surface. If I had questions for the mirror then, I do not remember them now. At twenty, the reflection seemed a kiss given by a close friend; on the surface, all was smooth, clear. I had no questions for the mirror then. I began to read for meaning at thirty, the reflective surface a lover presuming to know the whole story. If I had a question then, it was why, not how. At forty, there were clear lines to follow. When was the question, the question was when. At fifty, nothing is as smooth or clear, but there are more lines to follow.

The Calculus of Freedom

The rescued eagle hates his aviary,
an expansive habitat according to the sign
directing visitors to keep a safe distance. He is restive
in his tree-lined cage. His glittering eyes,
diamond-tip precision instruments
in the mathematics of attack and survival,
dart from one angle to another, taking the measure
of his territory. He studies the sky,
which he must see through wire mesh
as fractals of hexagonal blue, points of reference
he seems to count in quick clicks
of eye and neck movements, until he fixes
upon the longest branch of the spreading oak tree,
supporting axis of his enclosure.
Even with a broken wing, he is elegant
with purpose, exploding into flight.
Listing at 45 degrees to pain, he keeps his eyes
on one point—the point of greatest resistance—
and alights in perfect equilibrium, testing the limb
like the bow of a violin, having calculated precisely
the dimensions of his captivity.

Seizing the Day

On this one day
finite as a glass cube,
within which you do not plan
past this hour, you are traveling only
as far as daylight will take you. Inside the car,
the autumn sun, infused with white light
and a little heat,
strokes the windshield; just ahead,
the peaked shade of mountains.

You are listening to a top-one-hundred countdown
on the radio. She says, *Satisfaction*
will be on top—*Satisfaction*
always is.

As you sear these roads in your haste
to get somewhere you have never been before,
you notice the leisurely pace of other lives
in their familiar routines: how an old man,
digging in his mailbox for news of a world
he doesn't believe in, stares at you
hurtling past,
a wave of music and light,
with the hooded eyes of envy.

And how a young couple facing each other
at the window of a small café
raise their glasses of wine to their lips, oblivious
to the way, flashing by, you have stolen their souls
with your eyes.

To Understand El Azul

We dream in the language we all understand,
in the tongue that preceded alphabet and word.
Each time we claim beauty from the world,
we approximate its secret grammar, its silent
syntax; draw nearer to the Rosetta stone
for dismantling Babel.

If I say *el azul,* you may not see the color
of *mi cielo, mi mar.* Look once upon my sky,
my sea, and you will know precisely
what *el azul* means to me.

Begin with this: the cool kiss
of a September morning in Georgia, the bell-shaped
currents of air changing in the sky, the sad ghosts
of smoke clinging to a cleared field, and the way
days will taste different in your mouth each week
of the season. *Sábado*: Saturday
is strawberry. *Martes*: Tuesday
is bitter chocolate to me.

Do you know what I mean?

Still, everything we dream circles back.
Imagine the bird that returns home every night
with news of a miraculous world just beyond
your private horizon. To understand its message,
first you must decipher its dialect of distance,
its idiom of dance. Look for clues
in its arching descent, in the way it resists
gravity. Above all, you have to learn why
it aims each day

toward the boundless *azul.*

The Names of the Dead: An Essay on the Phrase

*The functions of the human body are phrased this way: the heart beats
and rests; the lungs fill and subside; muscles demand rest from effort,
as sustained tension results quickly in exhaustion.*
FROM *THE ART OF MAKING DANCES* BY DORIS HUMPHREY

We live by the phrase. We long for the order of declaration and pause. The
functions of the human body are phrased this way: the heart beats and
rests; the lungs fill and subside. Outside of the body, in the general world
of matter, tension and relaxation also operate as a law; this counterpoint
of energy and loss is inescapable as a pattern. *Scenes of chaos and destruc-
tion evocative of the nightmare world of Hieronymus Bosch,* reported the
New York Times, *with smoke and debris blotting out the sun. But the real
carnage was concealed by the twisted, smoking, ash-choked carcasses of the
structures. There were hundreds of people on the street waiting for the names
of the dead. There is nothing anybody can do,* a firefighter replied, *nothing
anybody can do.* In long stretches of unphrased movement, the kinesthetic
link of our bodies with an event is sometimes lost. This counterpoint of
energy and loss. Outside of the body. *Scenes of chaos and destruction.* In
the general world of matter. *There is nothing anybody can do.* Confronted
with the loss. The heart beats and rests. *With smoke and debris blotting out
the sun.* The lungs fill and subside. *Concealed by the twisted, smoking, ash-
choked carcasses of the structures.* Muscles of the heart demand rest from
continued effort. *But the real carnage was concealed. Nothing anybody can
do.* We long for the order of declaration and pause. Inescapable as a pattern.
This counterpoint of energy and loss. *The names of the dead.*

Ce

In long stretches of unphrased movement, the kinesthetic link of our bodies
with an event is sometimes lost. Confronted with the loss, the heart beats
and rests; the lungs fill and subside. According to the Times, *Washington
struggled to regain a sense of equilibrium; with warplanes crossing overhead,
national security officials discussed the possibility of a declaration of war.*

Long sentences leave us breathless and tired. Sustained tension results quickly in exhaustion. The heart beats and rests; the lungs fill and subside. *The possibility of a declaration of war. There is nothing anybody can do.* And the very short statement is also unsatisfactory: *The search is under way for those behind these evil acts,* the President said. *The resolve of our great nation is being tested.* Here the rests are too frequent; the breath is too short and therefore unfulfilling. *This is a difficult time for America,* he said. The heart beats and rests, beats and rests. *Nothing anybody can do.* The lungs fill and subside, fill and subside. *With warplanes crossing overhead. The search is under way. Nothing anybody can do. The names of the dead.*

☙

Outside of the body, in the general world of matter, tension and relaxation also operate as a law; this counterpoint of energy and loss is inescapable as a pattern. *There were refugees everywhere,* said the Times. *A memorial was set up. Long sheets of brown paper taped to the ground. Repeated on almost every one the single word, why? There were hundreds of pieces of paper in the air. A woman grabbed my hand,* said a passerby. *She was saying the Lord's Prayer. It was late in the afternoon. Hundreds of people on the street watching the stubs of the buildings burn. Hundreds of people on the street. Paper in the air. Late in the afternoon. Waiting for the names of the dead. A single word, repeated.*

Outside of the body. *Nothing anybody can do. Scenes of chaos and destruction. Late in the afternoon.* In the general world of matter. *The real carnage was concealed. A woman grabbed my hand. With warplanes overhead. Smoke and debris blotting out the sun.* The kinesthetic link. *She was saying the Lord's Prayer. Long sheets of brown paper.* Long stretches of unphrased movement. Long sentences. The inescapable pattern. *Late in the afternoon. A single word, repeated. The nightmare world of Hieronymus Bosch. Nothing anybody can do.* This counterpoint of energy and loss. *The evil acts. The resolve. A difficult time. Nothing anybody can do. America.* The names of the dead.

Gifts

Look what I have brought you from my walk
on the beach of my childhood. The memory of a conch shell,
polished by sand and seawater to a luminous smoothness,
stained by time and tide to an intimate pink. See how it spirals,
winding out of its simple design into a mystery? I was small
the day I found it. Someone had me firmly by the hand. The waves
were taller than I, and the sea seemed too dark blue, *azul-sangre,*
like the blood in veins. *Un mar furioso,* stay close, I had been warned—
only I had already spotted the pretty *concha*—just out of reach.
And I had to have it. I had to break the hold on me. I had to dig
the treasure out of the sodden, shifting sands
that almost took me. The sea slapped me hard
for what I stole from her. I was also scolded for my recklessness,
for bringing *algo salao* into the house,
more anger, the bad luck of things
                            spewed by the sea.

I understood nothing
about the search for truth and beauty then, and nothing
about what makes the world more than it is. I only knew I had to look
deep into the strangely exciting convolutions
of that marvelous *caracol,* to inhale its briny perfume, and to hear
the sound of my own blood magnified, echoed back to me, after
                            it had tasted red.

And here is a river stone,
not the thing itself, but the groove it left behind
on the moist red clay, preserved under layers of sweet pine straw
until today. But it was many years ago, a hot day in late June,
when I followed school friends to a secret place far from the paved road,
hidden by kudzu-draped acres of hardwood and pine, a pond fed

by an artesian well from an underground source, a meeting place
   unknown
to anyone, or so we thought, under or over the age of desire, where I
   learned,
as I stood apart, paralyzed by the howls of joy, witnessing the power
of the naked body in water, knowing, not this I know now, only that
I could not then, at fifteen,
take my clothes off in front of others, or even go anywhere near
                                             their easy abandon.

                      It was not as simple as modesty. My buttons
simply would not be undone; zippers caught my hair and tore
at my flesh. There was no letting go, no escaping the layers of cotton,
nor the voice inside my head proclaiming my body's imperfections
in a language my new friends did not need to know.
                                             And the stone
came home with me, slipping inside my pocket, and later rolled onto my
   bed,
imprinting its shape on my back, like a thumbprint, causing in me
a lingering unease, like a premonition: *algo, algo sin nombre,*
making me unhappy, keeping me awake.

I will give you this too:
Lightning tearing asunder the night sky
and striking the Banyan tree at my bedroom window—how I saw
its limbs outlined in red like candles on a birthday cake
through my closed lids, and how bolting straight out of a dream,
I found myself in my baby's room.
                                      I swear,
at that moment, I was more awake than I have ever been,
yet I have no memory of the awakening, or of how I must have raced the
   storm
in the dark—only of finding myself enfolding that beating heart, *mi niña,*
and of pressing her sweet flesh into the remembered curve

of my body, wishing I could make us one again, so that the earth,
if it were to split open to its molten core,

                            should swallow us together.

Finally, please also take the impetus for this poem. It was a gift
given me, I now pass on to you: an ancient word I came upon: *Relict.*
Consisting mainly of nuance and suggestion, this word
is rarely used in the present except by a few scholars specializing

                    in the traces and indentations
left in the natural world by living things now gone forever.
The sound it makes is beautiful to my ear. *Relict.*
A word whose oldest meanings derive from the Latin *relinquere,*
which means to leave behind, and, also,
in a usage now listed as archaic,
something left unchanged.

THREE

A Love Story

El Amor: *A Story Beginning in Spanish*

Dos palomas en la ventana—two doves cooing and fluttering their wings on the window ledge draw me away from my work to witness the little drama unfolding below: a man in black pacing outside a café, smoking a cigarette he holds between thumb and index finger, inhaling deeply once, twice, *un gran suspiro*, then crushing it balletically under the toe of the black mirror of his shoe. He smells his hands, runs his fingers through pomaded hair, lights another. He glances at his watch. He does not yet see her moving in slow, seductive *bolero* tempo toward him. Red dress, red purse, red mouth—substantial hips and ass, hard little cones of breasts pointing straight ahead—a body strong and firm as any promise made by any woman to any man in the entire history of sex, she is a pendulum in tune with the turning of the world. On first sight of his *destino*, his body tenses like that of a Flamenco dancer poised to stomp his way into her *corazón*. Her pace slows even more under his gaze, her hips and purse synchronizing their swing and sway. Then, tossing her glossy mane, smoothing down her dress over her curves, five paces away, she stops. *¿Entonces, qué pasa, amigos?* Propelled forward by a command he thinks comes straight from his heart— but, friends, it was scripted into his cells long before he knew he would be born a man, not just any man, but *el hombre*, the one destined to possess this *mujer*—he grabs her arm and they lock steps and exit my field of vision. I sway over space trying to see what happens next, nearly losing my grasp and frightening the *palomas*, which soar off into the darkening sky, one in close pursuit of the other. And I am caught in the moment, *el instante, amigos*, when any story, in any language, anywhere in the world, may begin, at any time: suspended *aquí*—somewhere between desire and death.

ABOUT THE AUTHOR

Judith Ortiz Cofer is the author of the novel *The Meaning of Consuelo* (Farrar, Straus & Giroux, 2003) and of *Woman in Front of the Sun: On Becoming a Writer*; *The Latin Deli* (awarded the Anisfield-Wolf Book Award); *Silent Dancing* (recipient of a PEN/Martha Albrand Special Citation); *The Line of the Sun*; *Terms of Survival*; and *Reaching for the Mainland*. A collection of her short stories, *An Island Like You: Stories of the Barrio*, was named a Best Book of the Year (1995–96) by the American Library Association and was also awarded the first Pura Belpré medal by REFORMA of the ALA in 1996. She has also received the Christ-Janer Award in Creative Research from the University of Georgia; a residency in Bellagio, Italy, awarded by the Rockefeller Foundation; and fellowships from the National Endowment for the Arts and the Witter Bynner Foundation for poetry. In 2001, she was Vanderbilt University's Gertrude and Harold S. Vanderbilt Visiting Writer in Residence. Judith Ortiz Cofer lives with her family in Georgia. She is the Franklin Professor of English and Creative Writing at the University of Georgia.